MLS
SUPERSTARS

CHRIS WONDOLOWSKI

LANDON DONOVAN

CELEBRATE!

MATT REIS

THIERRY HENRY

Beach Ball Books

Published by Beach Ball Books LLC
Santa Barbara, Calif.
www.beachballbooks.com

Produced by Shoreline Publishing Group LLC
Santa Barbara, California
www.shorelinepublishing.com
President/Editorial Director: James Buckley, Jr.
Designed by Tom Carling, www.carlingdesign.com

All photographs, including cover, courtesy of Getty Images Sport.

ISBN: 978-1-936310-30-2

10 9 8 7 6 5 4 3 2 1   09 10 11 12 13

This book conforms to CPSIA 2008.

Printed through Asia Pacific, China. December, 2012.

Contents

PPL Park

THIS IS SOCCER   THIS IS SOCCER

2012 All-Star Game

Welcome to MLS

Soccer is the world's favorite sport . . . and Major League Soccer is North America's favorite soccer league! With 19 teams in the United States and Canada, MLS thrills fans in person and on TV. Along with great stars from around the world (see box), MLS teams showcase America's and Canada's top players for their hometown fans.

Speaking of fans, they have become one of the biggest stories in MLS in recent seasons. With great new stadiums opening up in many cities, fans have flocked to watch their heroes. Some cities have just gone crazy for soccer.

In Seattle, just about every game is a sellout. A parade of fans walks through downtown on the way to the stadium, gathering in followers as they go. In Portland, fans scream louder than the chainsaw that cuts a piece of a giant log after every Timbers goal. Though Portland only joined MLS in

THE WORLD OF MLS

More than 150 players from countries around the world travel to North America to play. In 2012, more than 65 nations sent players to MLS. Here are just a few of the international heroes helping their MLS clubs:

PLAYER, MLS CLUB	HOME COUNTRY
David Beckham, Galaxy	England
Thierry Henry, Red Bulls	France
Juninho, Galaxy	Brazil
Kei Kamara, Sporting K.C.	Sierra Leone
Rafa Marquez, Red Bulls	Mexico
Fredy Montero, Sounders	Colombia
Darlington Nagbe, Timbers	Liberia
Patrick Nyarko, Fire	Ghana
Mauro Rosales, Sounders	Argentina
Alvaro Saborio, Real Salt Lake	Costa Rica

STICKERS!

In the center of this book, you'll find two sheets of stickers. Find the team logos on the pages ahead. Then put the right team stickers there. Use the extra stickers to decorate your notebook or bedroom door. Have fun!

2011, the Timbers Army (which the fans call themselves) has made its name as one of the loudest and most loyal fan groups. They're not alone, though. In Kansas City, fans at one end of LIVESTRONG Sporting Park sit in The Cauldron . . . or should we say stand, since they don't sit down at all! Since Toronto FC joined MLS in 2007, its fans have almost never stopped yelling! Wearing red clothing like their club, the fans pack every

The Portland lumberjack "Timber Joey" saws off a disk of wood after every goal scored by the Timbers.

MLS action is intense! Players such as Chance Myers of Sporting KC (left) and Wilman Conde of the Red Bulls need great fitness to run for the full 90 minutes.

game. Non-stop singing, flag-waving, and cheering are as much a part of Toronto FC games as corner kicks.

Those are just a few examples. At every MLS stadium, face-painted fans young and old love MLS soccer action.

The MLS regular season runs from "First Kick" in March until late October. Each team plays 34 games. Then, the MLS playoffs begin in late October. The 10 teams—five each from the Eastern and Western Conferences—with the most points earn spots in the playoffs. When four teams remain, the Conference Championships are played as a pair of two-game series. The winners earn a spot in the MLS Cup! Starting in 2012, the MLS Cup is held in the city whose conference champion had the most regular-season points.

Next up: Take a trip through MLS history, and then meet the best players on every team . . . plus, have fun with stickers!

Kickoff!

In 1994, the United States played host to the World Cup. Soccer fans from around the globe traveled to U.S. cities to watch the world's best national teams play. But millions of American fans also came to the games. Soccer had never been more popular. From that excitement for the game came Major League Soccer, which started in 1996. Ten teams began play that first season in cities from New York to Los Angeles. American stars such as Cobi Jones, Eric Wynalda, Brad Friedel, and Alexi Lalas continued the success they had had at the World Cup. International stars such as Colombia's Carlos Valderrama (the first MVP) and Mexican goalie Jorge Campos also joined the new league. D.C. United won the first MLS Cup.

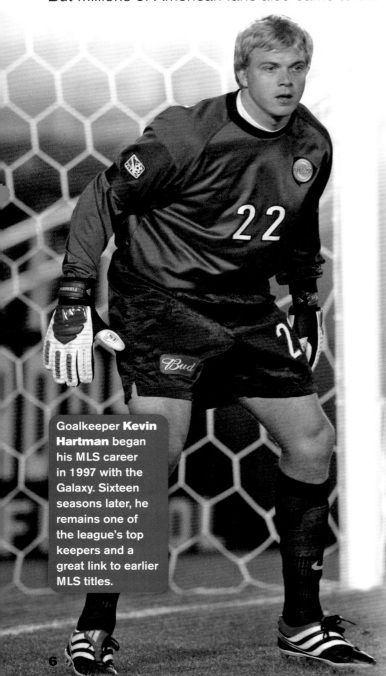

Goalkeeper **Kevin Hartman** began his MLS career in 1997 with the Galaxy. Sixteen seasons later, he remains one of the league's top keepers and a great link to earlier MLS titles.

MLS CUP CHAMPIONS

YEAR	WINNER
2012	_____
2011	L.A. Galaxy
2010	Colorado Rapids
2009	Real Salt Lake
2008	Columbus Crew
2007	Houston Dynamo
2006	Houston Dynamo
2005	LA Galaxy
2004	D.C. United
2003	San Jose Earthquakes
2002	L.A. Galaxy
2001	San Jose Earthquakes
2000	Kansas City
1999	D.C. United
1998	Chicago Fire
1997	D.C. United
1996	D.C. United

Early Season Success

By 2000, MLS had grown to 12 teams in three divisions. Fans continued to support the league. Some clubs averaged more than 17,000 fans at each game. Some clubs drew far more! The Los Angeles Galaxy helped put MLS on the international map in 2000. They won the CONCACAF Champions League, beating out top pro teams from North and Central America and the Caribbean. American star Landon Donovan led the San Jose Earthquakes to their first MLS Cup in 2001. San Jose won again in 2003, helped by an amazing comeback in the playoffs that included a win on a golden goal! In 2004, D.C. United won after its own three-goal comeback in a conference final that they won on penalty kicks.

Growing!

In 2005, MLS added two new clubs: Real Salt Lake and Chivas USA. Chivas was part of a unique team-up with a club from the Mexican League of the same name. Based in Los Angeles, Chivas USA showed how popular MLS had become with the many Hispanic fans living in the States. In 2007, the league expanded again, this time to the north. Toronto FC became the first Canadian MLS team. Its fans quickly became among the most loyal—and loud—in the league! They would be joined by the Vancouver Whitecaps in 2011 and the Montreal Impact in 2012.

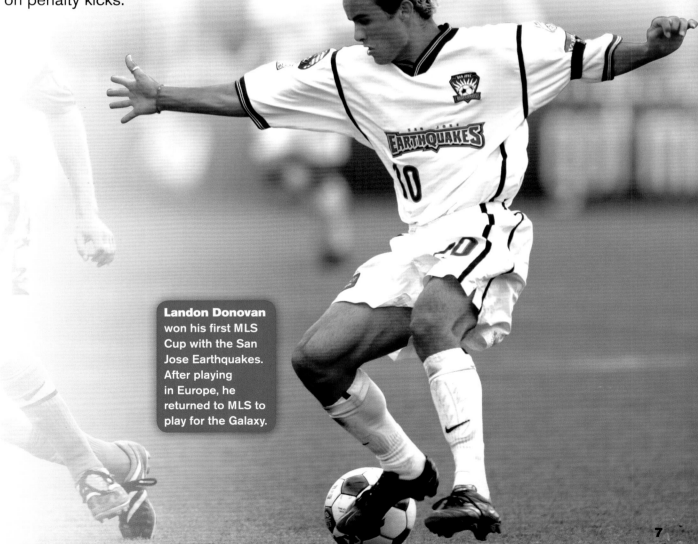

Landon Donovan won his first MLS Cup with the San Jose Earthquakes. After playing in Europe, he returned to MLS to play for the Galaxy.

Here Comes Beckham!

The other big news in 2007 came from Europe. David Beckham, the former captain of the English national team and one of the world's most famous players, joined the L.A. Galaxy. His arrival energized the entire league. Millions watched the press conference announcing his arrival.

In 2008, the Columbus Crew won its first MLS Cup ever! The Crew was one of the original teams in the league.

MLS Grows Again!

Soccer has always been very popular in the Northwest United States. In 2009, the MLS welcomed Seattle Sounders FC and their excited fans. The Sounders have become one of the league's most popular clubs. In 2010, the Philadelphia Union joined MLS, bringing another strong team to the East Coast. And in 2011, back in the Northwest, the Portland Timbers played its first season.

Fans such as these in Toronto bring excitement—and lots of noise!—to every MLS game.

Look for more soccer action in the years ahead from teams such as Chivas USA (stripes) and the L.A. Galaxy.

What's Next?

MLS has 19 teams in two countries for the 2013 season. Top American players are joined by international stars such as Thierry Henry of France and the Red Bulls, former MVP David Ferreira of Colombia and FC Dallas, and goalie Donovan Ricketts of Jamaica and the Timbers.

Most teams now play in stadiums built just for soccer. The Houston Dynamo moved into BBVA Compass Stadium in 2012, for example. In all the stadiums, loyal fans cheer, sing, wave their scarves and banners, and provide great support for their favorites. If you haven't been to an MLS game . . . try to check one out in person! There's nothing like the excitement and celebration of a major pro soccer match. If you can't get to a game, you can watch MLS matches on TV on the NBC Sports Networks and ESPN. For lots more information about Major League Soccer, check out **www.mlssoccer.com**.

ALL-STARS!

The annual MLS All-Star Game features the top players in the league, but MLS adds a special treat for fans. In many seasons, the best MLS players face off not against each other but against national and world stars. Here are the results of all the MLS All-Star Games:

YEAR	SCORE
2013	_____
2012	MLS 3–Chelsea 2
2011	Manchester United 4–MLS 0
2010	Manchester United 5–MLS 2
2009	MLS 1–Everton 1*
2008	MLS 3–West Ham 2
2007	MLS 2–Celtic 0
2006	MLS 1–Chelsea 0
2005	MLS 4–Fulham 1
2004	East 3–West 2
2003	MLS 3–Guadalajara 2
2002	MLS 3–US Natl. Team 2
2001	West 6–East 6
2000	East 9–West 4
1999	West 6–East 4
1998	USA 6–World 1
1997	East 5–West 4
1996	East 3–West 2

*Everton 4-3 in penalty kicks.

Eddie Johnson (third from left) celebrates after his goal gave the MLS All-Stars the victory over Chelsea in 2012.

The Teams of
Major League Soccer

19 Teams . . . 19 Superstars!
Meet some of the top players on each Major League Soccer team!

 Chicago Fire

 New England Revolution

 Chivas USA

 New York Red Bulls

 Colorado Rapids

 Philadelphia Union

 Columbus Crew

 Portland Timbers

 D.C. United

 Real Salt Lake

 FC Dallas

 San Jose Earthquakes

 Houston Dynamo

 Seattle Sounders FC

 Los Angeles Galaxy

 Sporting Kansas City

 Impact Montréal

 Toronto FC

 Vancouver Whitecaps FC

Chicago Fire

Patrick Nyarko plays his sixth season with Chicago in 2013. A speedy and dependable midfielder, the native of Ghana has scored in each of his MLS seasons.

HOME CITY **Chicago, IL**
STADIUM **Toyota Park**
FIRST SEASON **1998**
MLS CUP TITLES **1**

QUICK KICK
The Fire celebrated its 15th anniversary in 2012 with a star-studded event including more than 20 former stars!

In 2011, his first full season in the Chivas USA net, **Dan Kennedy** was named the team MVP! The former UC Santa Barbara star also has played pro soccer in Chile.

CHIVAS STAR FACTS

▶ The team's full name is Club Deportivo Chivas USA, which means Sports Club Chivas USA.

▶ Chivas USA joined MLS in 2005 as an expansion team.

▶ The club shares the Home Depot Center with the L.A. Galaxy. It's the only such shared stadium in MLS.

▶ Local fans can see their Chivas USA heroes in action when the team heads out into Los Angeles for "Practice in the Community" sessions.

▶ Chivas USA leaders have won two MLS Coach of the Year awards: Bob Bradley (2006) and Preki (2007).

HOME CITY **Los Angeles, CA**
STADIUM **Home Depot Center**
FIRST SEASON **2005**
MLS CUP TITLES **0**

QUICK KICK
"Chivas" means "goat" in Spanish. The team's Mexican League partner is one of that country's most popular clubs.

Colorado Rapids

HOME CITY **Commerce City, CO**
STADIUM **Dick's Sporting Goods Park**
FIRST SEASON **1996**
MLS CUP TITLES **1**

RAPIDS STAR FACTS

▶ A bicycle kick by Rapids star Marcelo Balboa in 2000 was named the MLS Goal of the Year.

▶ Colorado's MLS Cup win in 2010 came after a dramatic overtime goal by Macoumba Kandji.

▶ The Rapids' fan Bulldog Supporters Club sometimes travels by bus to away games. The PID Army is well-known for its Rapids songs.

▶ The Rapids have four mascots! Each represents an animal that lives in the Rocky Mountains: Edson the Eagle, Marco Von Bison, Jorge El Mapache (which means raccoon), and Franz the Fox.

▶ The Rapids play their MLS neighbor, Real Salt Lake, for the Rocky Mountain Cup.

QUICK KICK
The Rapids play their home games more than a mile above sea level!

Jaime Castrillón joined the Rapids in 2012 as an International Player. The midfielder from Colombia quickly became a fan favorite and was among team leaders in goals.

13

Columbus Crew

CREW STAR FACTS

▶ The club got its name from a fan contest. A man named Luis Orozco suggested "Crew" and everyone loved the idea!

▶ Just three years after joining MLS in its first season, the Crew led the league in attendance in 1999.

▶ In 2008, Guillermo Barros Schelotto led Columbus to its first MLS Cup title. He was the MLS Cup MVP after he made a record three assists. He was also the first Crew player to be the league MVP.

▶ Thousands of Crew fans helped pack their home field for an important World Cup qualifying game in 2012. They watched the U.S. beat Jamaica, 1–0.

▶ Crew Stadium was also the home of the 2000 All-Star Game and the 2001 MLS Cup.

Speedy forward **Federico Higuaín** settled in Columbus in 2012 after his soccer world travels included stops in Turkey, Mexico, and his native Argentina.

HOME CITY **Columbus, OH**
STADIUM **Crew Stadium**
FIRST SEASON **1996**
MLS CUP TITLES **1**

QUICK KICK
Crew Stadium opened in 1999 as the first soccer-specific stadium in the United States.

D.C. United

UNITED STAR FACTS

▶ D.C. United won the first MLS Cup in 1996, defeating the San Jose Clash, 3–2, with a spectacular overtime, come-from-behind performance.

▶ The club's most recent MLS Cup title came in 2004. A 3–2 victory over the Kansas City Wizards capped off a season-ending streak that saw United win nine of its final 10 games.

▶ D.C. United came out on top in the Lamar Hunt U.S. Open Cup in 1996 and 2008.

▶ Four D.C. United stars earned MLS MVP honors: Marco Etcheverry (1998), Cristian Gómez (2007), Luciano Emilio (2008), and Dwayne DeRosario (2011).

▶ Talon the Eagle is the D.C. United mascot, flying all over the place to make appearances for the team.

▶ D.C. United represented MLS and U.S. soccer very well, winning the 1998 CONCACAF Champions Cup.

HOME CITY **Washington, DC**
STADIUM **RKF Stadium**
FIRST SEASON **1996**
MLS CUP TITLES **4**

Dwayne DeRosario had his best season in 2011. He won the Golden Boot as the MLS leading goalscorer (16) and was named the MLS MVP, too.

QUICK KICK
The four MLS Cups captured by D.C. United (most recent: 2004) are the most by any club in MLS history!

15

FC Dallas

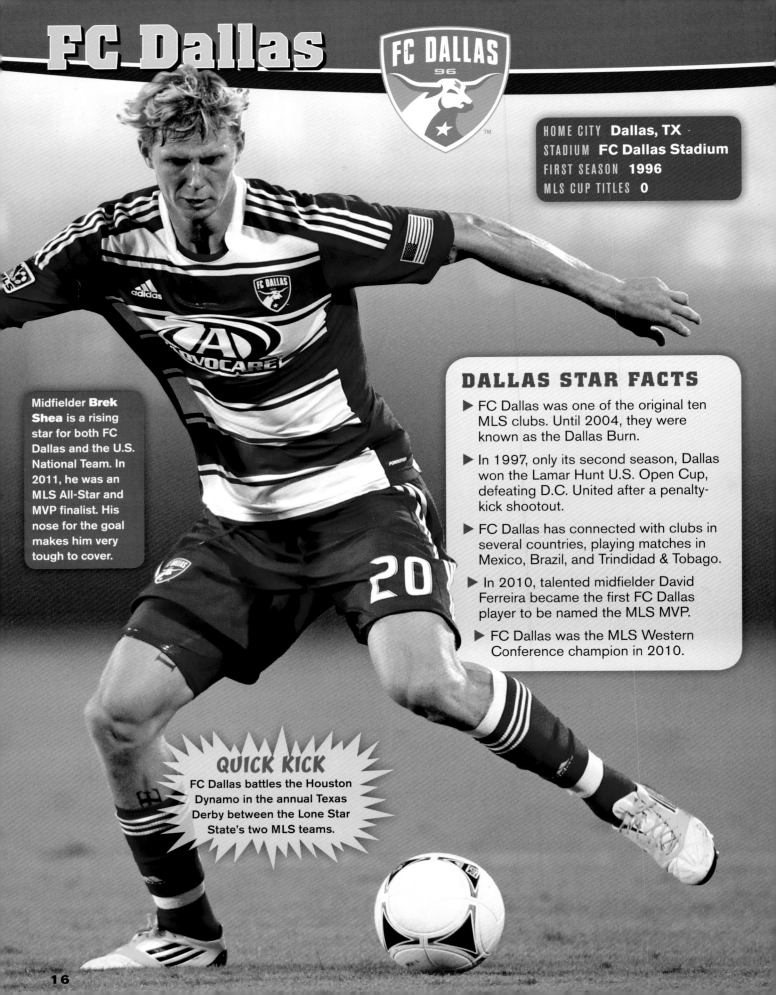

FC DALLAS
96 TM

HOME CITY **Dallas, TX**
STADIUM **FC Dallas Stadium**
FIRST SEASON **1996**
MLS CUP TITLES **0**

Midfielder **Brek Shea** is a rising star for both FC Dallas and the U.S. National Team. In 2011, he was an MLS All-Star and MVP finalist. His nose for the goal makes him very tough to cover.

DALLAS STAR FACTS

► FC Dallas was one of the original ten MLS clubs. Until 2004, they were known as the Dallas Burn.

► In 1997, only its second season, Dallas won the Lamar Hunt U.S. Open Cup, defeating D.C. United after a penalty-kick shootout.

► FC Dallas has connected with clubs in several countries, playing matches in Mexico, Brazil, and Trindidad & Tobago.

► In 2010, talented midfielder David Ferreira became the first FC Dallas player to be named the MLS MVP.

► FC Dallas was the MLS Western Conference champion in 2010.

QUICK KICK
FC Dallas battles the Houston Dynamo in the annual Texas Derby between the Lone Star State's two MLS teams.

Houston Dynamo

HOME CITY **Houston, TX**
STADIUM **BBVA Compass Stadium**
FIRST SEASON **1996**
MLS CUP TITLES **2**

DYNAMO STAR FACTS

▶ The Dynamo club started in 2006; the franchise was originally in San Jose, but moved to Texas.

▶ Like many MLS clubs, the Dynamo supports a large youth organization, sponsoring clubs down to the U-12 level for boys and girls.

▶ Houston has not one, but four large (and loud!) fan groups, led by the oldest, the Texian Army.

▶ The Dynamo became only the second MLS team ever to win back-to-back league championships. They won the MLS Cup in 2006 and repeated the feat in 2007.

▶ The Dynamo was the champion of the MLS Eastern Conference in 2011.

QUICK KICK
The annual BBVA Compass Cup pits the Dynamo against an international team for charity. Teams have come from Mexico, Spain, and England.

Midfielder **Brad Davis** has been with Houston since it began. He has won three team MVP awards and is the club's all-time leader in games and assists.

Los Angeles Galaxy

GALAXY STAR FACTS

▶ The Galaxians are the team's oldest supporters club. They have since been joined by the Riot Squad and the Angel City Brigade.

▶ Galaxy coach Bruce Arena holds the record for most wins while in charge of the U.S. National Team.

▶ The Galaxy won the U.S. Open Cup, a national tournament for teams at many levels, in 2001 and 2005.

▶ Galaxy players scored two MLS Goals of the Year: Carlos Ruiz in 2002 and Landon Donovan in 2009.

▶ The Galaxy won the 2011 MLS Cup in front of their home fans at the Home Depot Center.

Landon Donovan joined the Galaxy in 2005. He's the team's all-time leader in goals and assists. He played in three World Cups with the U.S. National Team.

HOME CITY **Los Angeles, CA**
STADIUM **Home Depot Center**
FIRST SEASON **1996**
MLS CUP TITLES **3**

QUICK KICK
The Galaxy have appeared in the MLS playoffs more often than any team in league history!

Montreal Impact

IMPACT STAR FACTS

▶ The Impact is the newest MLS club. Its first season was 2012.

▶ The team has been playing for much longer, however. The Impact won three titles in the American Professional Soccer League (also called the A-League) and also took part for many seasons in the United Soccer League.

▶ The Impact won the 2009 USL championship, defeating its future MLS partner, the Vancouver Whitecaps FC.

▶ Before joining MLS, the Impact won the 2008 Nutrilite Canadian Championship, defeating MLS's Toronto FC.

▶ French is the official language of Quebec, Montreal's Canadian province. The team's French motto is "Tous Pour Gagner," which means "Together for victory!"

HOME CITY **Montreal, Quebec**
STADIUM **Stade Saputo**
FIRST SEASON **2012**
MLS CUP TITLES **0**

Quebec native, Canadian national team star, and midfielder **Patrice Bernier** came home to Canada to lead the impact in 2012. He had previously played in Denmark, Norway, and Germany.

QUICK KICK
The Impact's home stadium is built on the same grounds where the 1976 Olympics were held in Montreal.

New England Revolution

HOME CITY **Foxboro, MA**
STADIUM **Gillette Stadium**
FIRST SEASON **1996**
MLS CUP TITLES **0**

Lee Nguyen might be one of the smallest players, but he's also one of the most talented. In 2012, his first MLS season, Nguyen was a key part of the Revolution's offense, using his speed and ball-control abilities.

REVOLUTION STAR FACTS

▶ The Revolution was one of the first clubs in MLS. U.S. star Alexi Lalas headlined the club's first season in 1996.

▶ In 2002, the Revs made the MLS Cup. Playing at home before the biggest crowd ever to see the game, they lost to the L.A. Galaxy on an overtime "golden goal."

▶ Clint Dempsey, now a key member of the U.S. National Team, was the MLS Rookie of the Year for New England in 2004.

▶ High-scoring forward Taylor Twellman was the first Revolution player to be named MLS MVP in 2005.

▶ In 2008, the Revolution became the first team to win the SuperLiga, a competition among North and Central American pro clubs.

QUICK KICK
The Revolution has won the Team Fair Play Award twice (2002 and 2008)!

RED BULLS STAR FACTS

▶ The New York City area has been home to an MLS club since the league's first season in 1996. The team was originally called the MetroStars.

▶ The team took on its current name in 2006 when an energy-drink company purchased the team.

▶ In a wild 2006 game, New York tied a record for most goals in a half (6) and set a mark for fastest 6 goals (only 32 minutes!).

▶ The Red Bulls boasted the best one-two scoring punch in MLS in 2012, as both Thierry Henry and Kenny Cooper were among the top five in goals scored.

HOME CITY **New York, NY**
STADIUM **Red Bull Arena**
FIRST SEASON **1996**
MLS CUP TITLES **0**

Thierry Henry is one of the MLS's most accomplished players. He helped France win the 1998 World Cup. In the English Premier League, he was a scoring champion for Arsenal.

QUICK KICK
The Red Bulls' Seth Stammler was the 2010 MLS W.O.R.K.S. Humanitarian of the Year.

Philadelphia Union

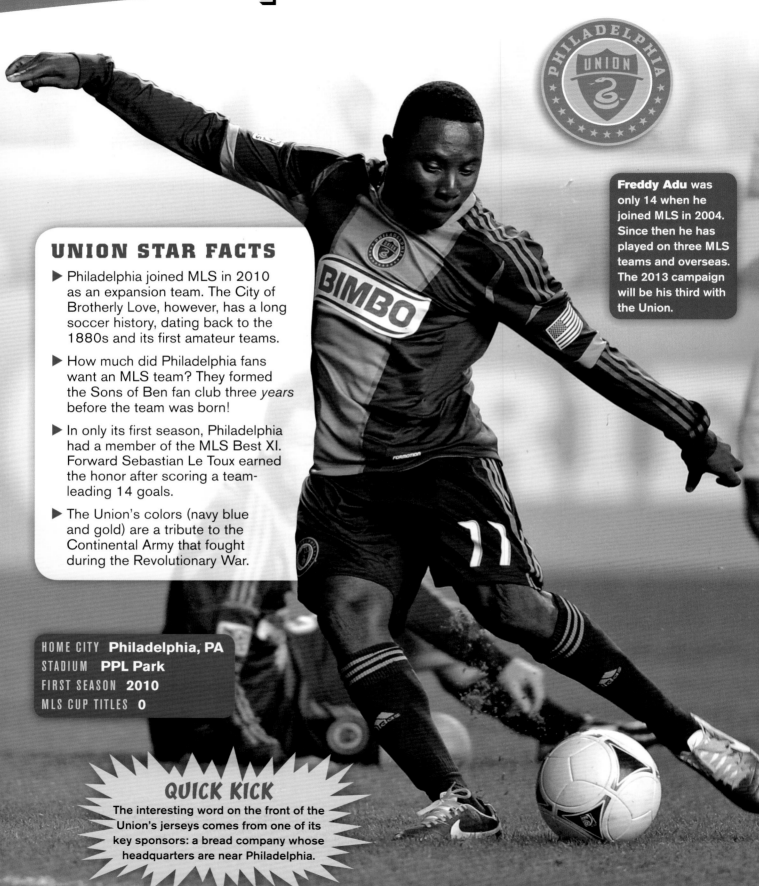

PHILADELPHIA UNION

Freddy Adu was only 14 when he joined MLS in 2004. Since then he has played on three MLS teams and overseas. The 2013 campaign will be his third with the Union.

UNION STAR FACTS

▶ Philadelphia joined MLS in 2010 as an expansion team. The City of Brotherly Love, however, has a long soccer history, dating back to the 1880s and its first amateur teams.

▶ How much did Philadelphia fans want an MLS team? They formed the Sons of Ben fan club three *years* before the team was born!

▶ In only its first season, Philadelphia had a member of the MLS Best XI. Forward Sebastian Le Toux earned the honor after scoring a team-leading 14 goals.

▶ The Union's colors (navy blue and gold) are a tribute to the Continental Army that fought during the Revolutionary War.

HOME CITY **Philadelphia, PA**
STADIUM **PPL Park**
FIRST SEASON **2010**
MLS CUP TITLES **0**

QUICK KICK
The interesting word on the front of the Union's jerseys comes from one of its key sponsors: a bread company whose headquarters are near Philadelphia.

HOME CITY	**Portland, OR**
STADIUM	**Jeld-Wen Field**
FIRST SEASON	**2011**
MLS CUP TITLES	**0**

Darlington Nagbe led the University of Akron to the 2010 NCAA soccer title and was named the top player in the country. With Portland, he has proven to be an exciting part of their offense.

TIMBERS STAR FACTS

▶ The Timbers have been a pro team since 1975. They played in the North American Soccer League and later were one of the top teams in the United Soccer League, before joining MLS in 2011.

▶ Portland's supporters are known as the Timbers Army and have quickly become one of the league's most well-known fan groups.

▶ Six months before First Kick 2011, Portland had sold out every seat at Jeld-Wen Field for 2012.

▶ The team's Stand Together program provides funds to help local youth sports and family events.

QUICK KICK

The log slabs cut by Timber Joey (see page 5) are given to the Timbers' goal scorers after each home game!

Real Salt Lake

HOME CITY **Salt Lake City, UT**
STADIUM **Rio Tinto Stadium**
FIRST SEASON **2005**
MLS CUP TITLES **1**

Look for Costa Rican forward **Álvaro Saborío** around the goal. In his first three seasons with RSL, he has never scored less than 14 goals in a year.

RSL STAR FACTS

▶ Real Salt Lake, often called RSL, joined MLS as an expansion team in 2005.

▶ RSL won its first MLS Cup in dramatic fashion in 2009. After they played the L.A. Galaxy to a 1–1 tie, Robbie Russell's penalty kick in the seventh round of a shootout gave RSL the championship.

▶ RSL's Rio Tinto Stadium played host to the 2009 MLS All-Star Game.

▶ RSL fans watch for the appearance of mascot Leonardo the Lion at home games.

QUICK KICK

Remember, Real is not pronouced "real" as in "seal," but "RAY-ahl," after the word's Spanish origins.

San Jose Earthquakes

No one in MLS has scored goals as often as forward **Chris Wondolowski** has in the past three seasons. The forward won the Golden Boot in 2012; he also won in 2010.

HOME CITY **San Jose, CA**
STADIUM **Buck Shaw Stadium**
FIRST SEASON **1996**
MLS CUP TITLES **2**

EARTHQUAKES STAR FACTS

▶ San Jose won its first MLS Cup in 2000, helped by a goal from young U.S. phenom Landon Donovan.

▶ In 2003, the Quakes won their second MLS Cup thanks to a late penalty save and a record-setting four goals.

▶ The original Quakes franchise moved to Houston in 2005. The current San Jose club started play again in 2008.

▶ Quakes goalies have won three MLS Goalkeeper of the Year awards: Joe Cannon (2002) and Pat Onstad (2003 and 2005).

▶ In 2010, Chris Wondolowski set an MLS record by scoring 10 straight goals for San Jose.

QUICK KICK

Two rival California teams, the Quakes and the L.A. Galaxy, play the California Clasíco games each season.

Seattle Sounders FC

SEATTLE
SOUNDERS FC

HOME CITY **Seattle, WA**
STADIUM **CenturyLink Field**
FIRST SEASON **2009**
MLS CUP TITLES **0**

Fredy Montero has been a star since helping Seattle kick off its first MLS season. He has set team points records and earned MLS All-Star selections.

SOUNDERS STAR FACTS

▶ Soccer-crazy Seattle welcomed the Sounders to MLS in 2009, the 15th MLS team.

▶ Sounders season ticket holders get to vote on some team decisions!

▶ The Sounders, who took their name from earlier pro teams in Seattle, are the only MLS team with a 53-piece band.

▶ Among the Sounders' owners: TV star Drew Carey and Microsoft co-founder Paul Allen.

▶ After Seattle's first three seasons, Fredy Montero was the team's all-time leader in goals and assists.

QUICK KICK
At Sounders' home games, listen for fans singing "Sounders 'Til I Die" at the 74th minute.

Sporting Kansas City

HOME CITY	**Kansas City, MO**
STADIUM	**Livestrong Sporting Park**
FIRST SEASON	**1996**
MLS CUP TITLES	**1**

Graham Zusi helped Maryland win two NCAA soccer titles, and he has helped Sporting with his solid midfield play. Zusi was a 2012 MLS All-Star.

QUICK KICK

Livestrong Sporting Park played host to a key World Cup qualifying game matching Guatemela and the United States.

SPORTING STAR FACTS

► This club began life as one of the first 10 MLS teams in 1996.

► In their 2000 MLS Cup championship season, Kansas City earned a host of awards. Tony Meola was the MLS Cup MVP and MLS Goalkeeper of the Year. Peter Vermes was MLS Defender of the Year. (Vermes later took over as head coach in 2009.)

► In 2004, Kansas City won the U.S. Open Cup, defeating the Chicago Fire.

► Led by a stingy defense that gave up the fewest goals in the league, Sporting had one of MLS's best records in 2012.

Toronto FC

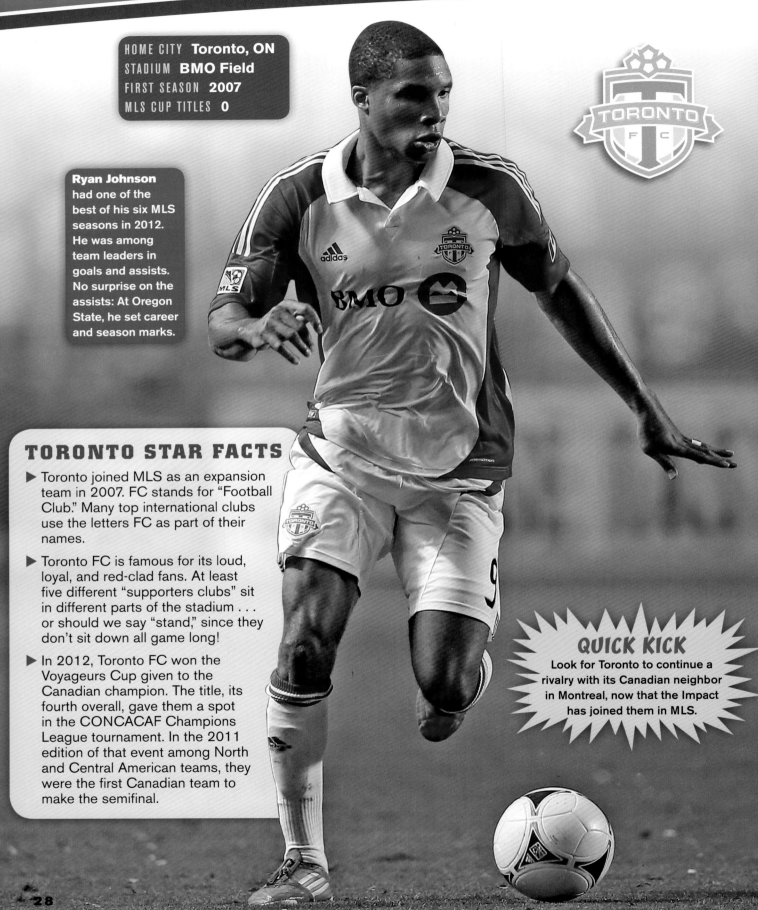

HOME CITY **Toronto, ON**
STADIUM **BMO Field**
FIRST SEASON **2007**
MLS CUP TITLES **0**

Ryan Johnson had one of the best of his six MLS seasons in 2012. He was among team leaders in goals and assists. No surprise on the assists: At Oregon State, he set career and season marks.

TORONTO STAR FACTS

▶ Toronto joined MLS as an expansion team in 2007. FC stands for "Football Club." Many top international clubs use the letters FC as part of their names.

▶ Toronto FC is famous for its loud, loyal, and red-clad fans. At least five different "supporters clubs" sit in different parts of the stadium . . . or should we say "stand," since they don't sit down all game long!

▶ In 2012, Toronto FC won the Voyageurs Cup given to the Canadian champion. The title, its fourth overall, gave them a spot in the CONCACAF Champions League tournament. In the 2011 edition of that event among North and Central American teams, they were the first Canadian team to make the semifinal.

QUICK KICK
Look for Toronto to continue a rivalry with its Canadian neighbor in Montreal, now that the Impact has joined them in MLS.

HOME CITY **Vancouver, BC**
STADIUM **BC Place**
FIRST SEASON **2011**
MLS CUP TITLES **0**

VANCOUVER
WHITECAPS
FC

WHITECAPS STAR FACTS

▶ The Whitecaps kicked off their first season in MLS by defeating rival Toronto FC. They repeated the feat by knocking off the new Montreal Impact in 2012's opening game!

▶ Keep an eye on young Whitecaps players Bryce Alderson and Caleb Clarke. These two young Canadians figure to be a part of Vancouver for a while, along with aiming for the Canadian national team.

▶ A Vancouver Whitecaps team also takes part in the women's W-League. These Whitecaps won the league title in 2004 and 2006.

Camilo arrived from Brazil in 2011 and was an immediate hit. He led the Whitecaps in goals in his first MLS season. This goal-hungry forward had also played in Malta and South Korea.

QUICK KICK
The Vancouver team was briefly known as the 86ers: That team started in 1986 and Vancouver was founded in 1886!

Soccer Stat City!

MLS MOST VALUABLE PLAYER

Year	Player	Team
2011	Dwayne De Rosario	D.C. UNITED
2010	David Ferreira	FC DALLAS
2009	Landon Donovan	L.A. GALAXY
2008	Guillermo Barros Schelotto	COLUMBUS CREW
2007	Luciano Emilio	D.C. UNITED
2006	Christian Gómez	D.C. UNITED
2005	Taylor Twellman	NEW ENGLAND REVOLUTION
2004	Amado Guevara	NEW YORK
2003	Preki	KANSAS CITY
2002	Carlos Ruiz	L.A. GALAXY
2001	Alex Pineda Chacón	MIAMI FUSION
2000	Tony Meola	KANSAS CITY
1999	Jason Kreis	DALLAS BURN
1998	Marco Etcheverry	D.C. UNITED
1997	Preki	KANSAS CITY
1996	Carlos Valderrama	TAMPA BAY MUTINY

MLS CUP WINNERS

YEAR	WINNER
2011	L.A. Galaxy
2010	Colorado Rapids
2009	Real Salt Lake
2008	Columbus Crew
2007	Houston Dynamo
2006	Houston Dynamo
2005	L.A. Galaxy
2004	D.C. United
2003	San Jose Earthquakes
2002	L.A. Galaxy
2001	San Jose Earthquakes
2000	Kansas City
1999	D.C. United
1998	Chicago Fire
1997	D.C. United
1996	D.C. United

100-GOAL SCORERS

Through the end of the 2012 season, the following players have scored at least 100 goals in MLS play. (* means they're still playing and adding to their total!)

PLAYER	GOALS
Jeff Cunningham	134
Jamie Moreno	133
Landon Donovan*	124
Ante Razov	114
Jason Kreis	108
Taylor Twellman	101
Dwayne De Rosario*	100

MLS GOALKEEPER OF THE YEAR

2011	Kasey Keller	SEATTLE SOUNDERS FC
2010	Donovan Ricketts	L.A. GALAXY
2009	Zach Thornton	CHIVAS USA
2008	Jon Busch	CHICAGO FIRE
2007	Brad Guzan	CHIVAS USA
2006	Troy Perkins	D.C. UNITED
2005	Pat Onstad	SAN JOSE EARTHQUAKES
2004	Joe Cannon	COLORADO RAPIDS
2003	Pat Onstad	SAN JOSE EARTHQUAKES
2002	Joe Cannon	SAN JOSE EARTHQUAKES
2001	Tim Howard	NEW YORK
2000	Tony Meola	KANSAS CITY
1999	Kevin Hartman	L.A. GALAXY
1998	Zach Thornton	CHICAGO FIRE
1997	Brad Friedel	COLUMBUS CREW
1996	Mark Dodd	DALLAS BURN

100 ASSISTS!

These helpful players dished out at least 100 assists in their careers. (* means he's still making perfect passes!

PLAYER	ASSISTS
Steve Ralston	135
Carlos Valderrama	114
Preki	112
Landon Donovan*	108
Jamie Moreno	102
Marco Etcheverry	101

100-WIN GOALKEEPERS

It's a team game, but having a great goalie leads to a lot of wins. Here are the MLS goalies who were in the nets for 100 or more wins. (* means they're still out there stopping shots.)

GOALKEEPER	WINS
Kevin Hartman*	179
Nick Rimando*	134
Zach Thornton	131
Joe Cannon*	116
Scott Garlick	107
Matt Reis*	103

Track the MLS 2012 Season and fill in the blanks below!

2012 MLS MOST VALUABLE PLAYER: _____ TEAM: _____

2012 MLS GOAL KEEPER OF THE YEAR: _____ TEAM: _____

2012 MLS CUP WINNER: _____

THANKS, FANS!

Thanks for cheering for your favorite MLS team!

See you at the match!